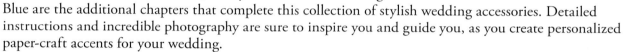

I've wanted to do a book like this for as long as I can remember.

I love beautiful things, and weddings are one of the most beautiful things we experience in life. So it really was a dream come true when I was asked to be part of such an incredibly beautiful book of paper-craft wedding projects!

Color is such a powerful and important element in any wedding. The six chapters in this book are each dedicated to a different color scheme and design style. From the exquisitely detailed elegance of the Magical Metallic suite (page 10) and the sleek sophistication of the Black Tie affair (page 4), to the subtle simplicities of the Earth Tones Suite (page 36), every collection features a unique combination of paper projects suited for all creative skill levels. Red Radiance, Pretty Pastels and Something Blue are the additional chapters that complete this collection of stylish wedding accessories. Detailed instructions and incredible photography are sure to inspire you and guide you, as you create personalized paper-craft accents for your wedding.

Many of the paper-craft brands and cutting-edge products that you know and love are featured in this book. You'll see these products come to life in the hands of Spellbinders' incredibly talented designers: Karen Taylor, Kimberly Crawford, Jennifer Davis, Linda Duke, Becca Feeken and Kazan Clark. It is a blessing to work with these beautiful women, and I am honored to share their incredible designs and creative spirits with you.

In every project you'll see how Spellbinders' one-of-a-kind Die & Embellishment Templates can help to transform your creative vision into breathtaking reality. From save-the-dates and invitations, to place cards, thank-you notes, and even bouquets, boutonnieres and centerpieces, finding the inspiration to create your dream wedding is just a few page turns away.

Congratulations on your upcoming wedding! May your beautiful day be only the beginning of a long, happy and inspiring life together!

Happy crafting,
Stacey

Stacey Caron

Stacey has been scrapbooking and stamping for a number of years, and her enthusiasm for paper crafts truly inspires others. She has instructed throughout the U.S. and internationally for retailers, private groups, scrapbook and stamping stores, distributors and sales rep groups. Prior to establishing Spellbinders, Stacey practiced dentistry for 11 years as a Registered Dental Hygienist. She and her husband Jeff have been married for 14 years and have two young sons, Nathan and Justin.

Contents

Black Tie

Magical Metallic

Pretty Pastels

Red Radiance

Earth Tones Suite

Something Blue

Black Tie

Designs by Kazan Clark, courtesy of Spellbinders

Thank You

Invitation

Cut a 12 x 6-inch piece of black card stock. With long side horizontal, score vertical lines 3 inches and 9 inches from one side. Fold along score lines to form base of gatefold card.

Cut two 5⅞ x 5⅞-inch squares from white card stock. Set one square aside.

Cut one 5¾ x 5¾-inch square from black card stock and one 5⅜ x 5⅜-inch square from Black Brocade printed paper. Layer white card-stock, black card-stock and printed-paper squares. Cut layered squares in half and adhere top and bottom edges to front of card base with center edges meeting.

Centered on each fold of card base, cut a slit the width of the black ribbon. Thread a length of white ribbon through slits, across the back of the card and over the front, extending ribbon ends slightly beyond center opening. Repeat with a length of black ribbon. With card closed, turn ribbon ends under center edges of layered squares and secure. Adhere remaining white card-stock square to inside of card back, covering ribbons.

Cut a label from glazed card stock using Labels Five No. 2 Die Template. Adhere label to a piece of white card stock, and then trim edges to form a neat border.

Edit and print photo of wedding rings on home printer or at a photo-printing store. Position Fancy Tags No. 2 Die Template over photograph and emboss using die-cutting machine. Trim along embossed edge and mount onto black card stock. Trim to form a neat border.

Cut and emboss a flourish tag die from iridescent white card stock using Fancy Tags No. 2 Die Template. Adhere bordered photo to tag. Embellish tag with rhinestones and adhere tag to label with adhesive foam dots.

Apply glue to half of label and attach to front of card.

Sources: Glazed card stock from Bazzill Basics Paper Inc.; Wedding printed paper from Making Memories; die templates from Spellbinders Paper Arts.

Materials
- **Card stock: white, white iridescent, black**
- **Raven Wallpaper glazed card stock**
- **Black Brocade Wedding printed paper**
- **Digital photo of wedding rings**
- **Satin ribbon: 1½-inch-wide black, ⅜-inch-wide white**
- **Clear rhinestones**
- **Nestabilities® Labels Five Die Templates (#S4-229)**
- **Shapeabilities® Fancy Tags Die Templates (#S4-235)**
- **Manual die-cutting machine**
- **Craft knife**
- **Adhesive foam dots**
- **Paper adhesive**
- **Computer and photo-editing software**

Materials

- Green card stock
- White printed paper
- Copic markers: Cadmium Yellow Y15, Grayish Olive G94, Blue Green BG09, Pea Green YG63
- ⅝-inch-wide black-and-white ribbon
- Green cotton-covered 20-gauge stem wire
- Green floral tape
- Nestabilities® Classic Scalloped Circles Large Die Templates (#S4-124)
- Shapeabilities® Assorted Leaves Die Templates (#S4-076)
- Manual die-cutting machine
- ⅝-inch circle punch
- Tweezers
- Wire cutters
- Needle-nose pliers
- Paper adhesive

Boutonniere

Using Assorted Leaves Die Template and green card stock, cut and emboss two leaves. Ink die-cut leaves using markers and set aside.

Using Classic Scalloped Circle Large No. 4 Die Template and white printed paper, cut three circles. Punch two ⅝-inch circles from white printed paper.

To create flower, fold each scalloped circle in half and cut along fold. Fold each half in half again and cut along fold, making four segments, or petals, from each circle, for a total of 12 petals. Gripping each petal with tweezers, gently twist petal around tweezers to curl.

Make a small hole in center of each punched circle. Divide petals into two piles. Adhere six petals to each punched circle, overlapping slightly, by applying a small amount of adhesive to corner of petal. Let dry.

Stack two flowers on top of one another, and thread a 9-inch length of stem wire through center hole. Make a small loop at top of wire to secure, and then bend up lower end of wire behind flower to make the stem.

Position and adhere leaves behind flower; firmly wrap stem with floral tape. Tie a 10-inch length of ribbon in a bow around top of stem below flower.

Sources: Card stock from Bazzill Basics Paper Inc.; printed paper from ANW Crestwood/The Paper Company; Copic markers from Imagination International Inc.; die templates from Spellbinders Paper Arts.

Table Card

Cut an 6 x 8-inch piece of black card stock. Score across piece 1 inch from one narrow end.

Cut a second piece of black card stock to 6 x 7 inches. Apply adhesive to 1-inch scored flap on first piece and adhere two cards together to form an A-frame card.

Cut a 5¾ x 6¾-inch piece of printed paper and adhere to front of card.

Layer a 5 x 6-inch piece of black card stock and a 4¾ x 5¾-inch piece of white card stock. Wrap black satin ribbon around layered card stock, securing on back with tape. Tie ends in a large bow on front near top.

Using Labels Five No. 2 and No. 3 Die Templates, cut a label frame from printed paper. Mount onto black card stock and trim around edge to form a neat border.

Hand-print, or use a computer to generate, the word "Table" and the table number onto white card stock. Position Fancy Tags No. 2 Die Template over label and emboss using die-cutting machine. Trim along embossed edge and mount onto black card stock. Trim to form a neat border.

Using Fancy Tags No. 2 Die Template and white iridescent card stock, cut and emboss a flourish tag. Embellish with rhinestones.

Adhere tag to label and attach to front of table card with a foam dot.

Sources: Wedding printed paper from Making Memories; die templates from Spellbinders Paper Arts.

Materials
- **Card stock: white, white iridescent, black**
- **Black Brocade Wedding printed paper**
- **1½-inch-wide black satin ribbon**
- **Clear rhinestones**
- **Nestabilities® Labels Five Die Templates (#S4-229)**
- **Shapeabilities® Fancy Tags Die Templates (#S4-235)**
- **Manual die-cutting machine**
- **Craft knife**
- **Adhesive foam dots**
- **Paper adhesive**
- **Computer and printer (optional)**

Etched-Glass Favor

Cut a piece of self-adhesive vinyl large enough to cover votive holder. Use Classic Scalloped Circles Large No. 6 die template to cut circle from center area of vinyl piece. Set aside circle and apply vinyl with circle cutout to votive holder.

Cut a heart from self-adhesive vinyl using heart die template from In Spades Pendants. Position vinyl heart in middle of circle on votive holder.

Follow manufacturer's instructions to etch exposed areas of glass with etching cream. Remove etching cream and vinyl; dry glass surface.

Use Classic Scalloped Circles Large No. 5 Die Template to cut three scalloped circles from white printed paper. Punch two ⅝-inch circles from white printed paper.

Materials
- **Glass votive holder**
- **White printed paper**
- **Ribbon: ⅝-inch-wide black, ⅜-inch-wide white**
- **Glass-etching cream**
- **Clear self-adhesive vinyl**
- **Nestabilities® Classic Scalloped Circles Large Die Templates (#S4-124)**
- **Shapeabilities® In Spades Pendants Die Templates (#S4-208)**
- **Manual die-cutting machine**
- **⅝-inch circle punch**
- **Tweezers**
- **Adhesive dots**
- **Paper adhesive**

Assemble flower in the same manner as for boutonniere (page 7), securing stacked flowers with a dot of adhesive.

Wrap black ribbon around base of votive holder, trimming ends as needed so they overlap slightly. Adhere ends to secure.

Tie white ribbon over black ribbon, knotting to secure and trimming ends as desired. Secure flower in place with a dot of adhesive.

Sources: Card stock from Bazzill Basics Paper Inc.; printed paper from ANW Crestwood/The Paper Company; glass-etching cream from Armour Products; die templates from Spellbinders Paper Arts; adhesive dots from Glue Dots International.

Thank You Card

Form an 8½ x 5⅜-inch flat card from black card stock, and an 8¼ x 5⅛-inch flat card from white card stock.

Cut a strip of printed paper 8¼ x 2⅛ inches. Adhere strip onto black card stock and trim edges to form a neat border. Adhere layered strip to white flat card approximately ¼ inch from top.

Adhere black ribbon across front of layered strip, turning ends to back of white card and securing with tape. Repeat with white ribbon, centering it across black ribbon. Adhere white card to black card.

Using Labels Five No. 2 Die Template, cut a label from glazed card stock. Adhere to white card stock and trim to form a neat border.

Hand-print, or use a computer to generate, "Thank You" on white card stock. Position Fancy Tags No. 2 Die Template over sentiment and secure with low-tack tape. Cut and emboss die, using die-cutting machine.

Embellish tag with rhinestones and adhere to label with foam dots. Adhere finished label to card, centered on ribbon strip.

Sources: Glazed card stock from Bazzill Basics; Wedding printed paper from Making Memories; die templates from Spellbinders Paper Arts.

Materials
- **Card stock: white, white iridescent, black**
- **Raven Wallpaper glazed card stock**
- **Black Brocade Wedding printed paper**
- **Satin ribbon: 1½-inch-wide black, ⅜-inch-wide white**
- **Clear rhinestones**
- **Nestabilities® Labels Five Die Templates (#S4-229)**
- **Shapeabilities® Fancy Tags Die Templates (#S4-235)**
- **Manual die-cutting machine**
- **Craft knife**
- **Low-tack tape**
- **Adhesive foam dots**
- **Paper adhesive**
- **Computer and printer (optional)**

Magical Metallic

Designs by Becca Feeken, courtesy of Spellbinders

Couture Wedding Card

On scoring board, angle 12 x 12-inch piece of silver metallic card stock at 30 degrees. Score lines ½ inch apart, and then change orientation to opposite 30 degrees and score lines in same manner. Set aside.

Form a 6 x 8-inch top-folded card base from white card stock.

For card front, cut a 5¾ x 7¾-inch piece from silver metallic card stock; adhere to card front. Cut three 1½ x 7⅜-inch panels from scored silver metallic, and three 1¾ x 7⅝-inch panels from white card stock. Adhere scored silver panels on white panels. Use foam squares to adhere three layered panels to front of card, threading a length of silk ribbon under center and left panels before securing permanently. Place a pearl sticker at intersection of each scored line on scored panels. Tie ribbon ends in a bow.

Materials

- Card stock: white, silver metallic
- "Happily Ever After" rubber stamp
- Silver embossing powder
- Watermark ink pad
- Pearl stickers
- 1¼-inch-wide white silk ribbon
- Small silver brads
- Borderabilities® Classic Lace Border Grand Die Template (#S7-014)
- Nestabilities® Die Templates: Petite Scalloped Ovals Large (#S4-139), Petite Ovals Small (#S4-140)
- Shapeabilities® Die Templates: Flower Creations (#S4-072), Sunflower Set Two (#S4-158), Doodle Parts (#S4-121)
- Manual die-cutting machine
- Embossing heat tool
- Punches: scalloped photo corner, frond
- Scoring board and tool
- Transparent tape
- Adhesive foam squares
- Adhesive dots
- Computer and printer (optional)

Using Classic Lace Border Grand Die Template, cut and emboss two borders from white card stock. Adhere one end of one border to one end of second border with tape. Accordion-fold entire length of border. Adhere opposite ends together with tape to form a circle. Place adhesive dots on back of border at north, south, east and west points and attach to card base, easing into an oval shape. Use additional adhesive dots as needed to secure.

Using Petite Ovals Small Die Template, cut and emboss a 2¼ x 3½-inch oval from white card stock. Use watermark ink pad and rubber stamp to stamp sentiment on white oval; emboss with silver embossing powder. Embellish stamped design with pearl stickers.

Using Petite Scalloped Ovals Large Die Template, cut and emboss a slightly larger oval from silver metallic card stock. Adhere stamped white oval to silver oval with foam squares. Adhere silver oval to lace border with adhesive dots.

With white card stock, cut and emboss three sets of flowers using Flower Creations Die Templates, three small sunflowers using Sunflower Set Two Die Template, and two of the largest swirls using Doodle Parts Die Template. Punch six fronds from white card stock using frond punch.

Assemble three flowers by layering small center from Flower Creations on top of eight-petal flower from Flower Creations on top of small sunflower from Sunflower Set Two. Punch a hole in center of three layers and secure with a small silver brad. Use adhesive dots to adhere flowers vertically on remaining panel with two fronds behind each. Adhere one end of each spiral to panel, extending vertically from center flower. Place a small pearl on top of each brad in centers of flowers. Curl and shape petals to add dimension.

Cut a 5⅝ x 7½-inch piece from silver metallic; adhere to inside card back. Cut a 5 x 7¼-inch piece from white with hand-printed or computer-generated invitation text; adhere inside card over silver metallic. Use corner punch to cut four photo corners from silver metallic; adhere over corners of printed text panel.

Sources: Card stock from ANW Crestwood/The Paper Company and Wausau Paper; "Happily Ever After" rubber stamp from Hampton Art; Super Fine Detail embossing powder from Ranger Industries Inc.; Versamark watermark ink pad from Tsukineko Inc.; pearl stickers from Michaels Stores Inc.; silk ribbon from May Arts; die templates from Spellbinders Paper Arts; frond craft punch from Martha Stewart Crafts; scoring board and tool from Scor-Pal Products; adhesive dots from Glue Dots International.

Guest Memories Book

On scoring board, angle 12 x 12-inch piece of silver metallic card stock at 30 degrees. Score lines ½ inch apart, and then change orientation to opposite 30 degrees and score lines in same manner. Set aside.

Cut two pieces of chipboard each 8 x 6 inches, for front and back covers, and two pieces each 1 x 6 inches, for spines. Cover one side of each piece with white card stock, turning edges under and taping on underside.

Cut two pieces of printed paper each 9¼ x 5⅝ inches; set one piece aside. Adhere remaining piece to wrong side of one cover-and-spine set, overlapping edges of white card stock and creating an even border. There should be a space approximately ¼ inch wide between the cover and the spine.

For front cover, cut a 7¼ x 5½-inch piece of scored silver metallic card stock; adhere to center of front of remaining 8 x 6-inch cover. Cut a ¾ x 5¾-inch piece of scored silver metallic card stock; adhere to remaining 1 x 6-inch spine.

Using Classic Lace Border Grand Die Template, cut three lace borders from white card stock. Wrap one border around front book cover with lacey edge of border even with left edge of scored silver metallic card stock; tape ends on underside of cover. Tape remaining two lace borders end to end and accordion-fold entire piece. Tape opposite ends of folded border to make a circle. Adhere to front of book cover as shown in photo, coaxing shape into an oval.

Cut a 14-inch length of ribbon; center over oval lace border, turning end under at top edge and taping in

Materials

- **Card stock: white, silver metallic**
- **Coordinating printed paper**
- **"Happily Ever After" rubber stamp**
- **Silver embossing powder**
- **Watermark ink pad**
- **Chipboard**
- **Pearl stickers**
- **1¼-inch-wide white silk ribbon**
- **Borderabilities® Classic Lace Border Grand Die Template (#S7-014)**
- **Nestabilities® Die Templates: Petite Scalloped Ovals Large (#S4-139), Petite Ovals Small (S4-140)**
- **Manual die-cutting machine**
- **Embossing heat tool**
- **Scoring board and tool**
- **³⁄₁₆-inch hole punch**
- **Transparent tape**
- **Adhesive foam squares**
- **Adhesive dots**
- **Computer and printer (optional)**

place. Cut a 10-inch length of ribbon; position directly below 14-inch length, turning end under at bottom edge and taping in place.

Adhere front cover/spine set to back of reserved printed paper to cover raw edges of paper and ribbon, to create front book cover. Embellish front cover with pearl stickers.

Using Petite Scallop Ovals Large Die Template and silver metallic card stock, cut and emboss one 2½ x 3⅝-inch oval. Pull upper ribbon length down over lace border oval; adhere scallop oval to accordion folds of border, securing ribbon. Tie ends of ribbon in a bow below oval.

Using Petite Ovals Small Die Template and white card stock, cut and emboss a 2¼ x 3½-inch oval. Using watermark ink pad and "Happily Ever After" stamp, stamp onto white oval. Emboss with silver embossing powder. Adhere to silver scallop oval with adhesive foam squares. Embellish stamped oval with pearl stickers.

Hand-print, or use computer to generate desired number of pages (sample has 25 pages) measuring 8⅜ x 5½ inches with space for recording guest name, relationship to bride/groom, a favorite memory and the date.

On spines of front and back cover, punch holes 2 inches from each end and centered on spine. Punch corresponding holes on inner pages. Assemble pages between front and back cover and lace together with white ribbon.

Sources: Card stock from ANW Crestwood/The Paper Company and Wausau Paper; "Happily Ever After" rubber stamp from Hampton Art; printed paper from Die Cuts With A View; Super Fine Detail embossing powder from Ranger Industries Inc.; Versamark watermark ink pad from Tsukineko Inc.; pearl stickers from Michaels Stores Inc.; silk ribbon from May Arts; die templates from Spellbinders Paper Arts; scoring board and tool from Scor-Pal Products; adhesive dots from Glue Dots International.

Gatefold Thank You Card

On scoring board, angle 12 x 12-inch piece of silver metallic card stock at 30 degrees. Score lines ½ inch apart, and then change orientation to opposite 30 degrees and score lines in same manner. Cut a 5¼ x 1-inch panel and two 2½ x 5¼-inch panels. Set aside.

Cut an 11 x 5½-inch gatefold card base from white card stock. With long side horizontal, score lines at 2¾ inches and 8¼ inches from right-hand side; fold in side panels for gatefolds. Adhere a 5¼ x 5¼-inch metallic silver square inside card. Layer with a 5 x 5-inch square of white card stock. Adhere 5¼ x 1-inch scored panel across top of layered squares inside card. Adhere 2½ x 5¼-inch scored panels to front of card.

Using Petite Scalloped Ovals Large Die Template and silver metallic card stock, cut and emboss one 2⅜ x 3⅞-inch oval. Using Petite Ovals Small Die Template and white card stock, cut and emboss one 2¼ x 3⅜-inch oval. Stamp "Happily Ever After" rubber stamp with watermark ink pad onto white oval, omitting word portion; stamp "Thank You" between filigree borders. Emboss all with silver embossing powder. Adhere stamped oval to silver scalloped oval with foam squares. Adhere layered ovals to right front panel of card, overlapping left panel.

Materials
- Card stock: white, silver metallic
- Rubber stamps: "Happily Ever After," "Thank You"
- Silver embossing powder
- Watermark ink pad
- Pearl stickers
- Borderabilities® Classic Lace Border Grand Die Template (#S7-014)
- Nestabilities® Die Templates: Petite Scalloped Ovals Large (#S4-139), Petite Ovals Small (#S4-140)
- Shapeabilities® Die Templates: Flower Creations (#S4-072), Sunflower Set Two (#S4-158), Doodle Parts (#S4-121)
- Manual die-cutting machine
- Embossing heat tool
- Scoring board and tool
- Transparent tape
- Adhesive foam squares
- Adhesive dots

Adhere a foam square to opposite back side of oval to act as a spacer. ***Note:*** *Leave bottom portion of ovals free so band can slip underneath it.* Embellish card front and oval with pearl stickers.

For band, cut and layer a 12 x 1¾-inch white strip with a 12 x 1⅝-inch silver strip. Using Classic Lace Border Grand Die Template and white card stock, cut and emboss one border. Adhere over silver band strip. Fit band around card, overlapping ends at back and securing with adhesive. Embellish with pearl stickers.

Using Flower Creations Die Templates and white card stock, cut and emboss one each eight-petal and small five-petal flowers. Using Sunflower Set Two Die Template and white card stock, cut and emboss one small sunflower. Assemble flower by layering small five-petal and eight-petal flowers from Flower Creations with small sunflower; secure with a silver brad through center. Curl petals on top two layers toward front of flower, and petals on small sunflower toward back of flower. Adhere flower to right side of band.

Using Doodle Parts Die Template and white card stock, cut and emboss one of largest swirl. Use adhesive dot to adhere end of swirl behind flower, trimming to fit. Embellish band and center of flower with pearl stickers.

Fold card closed and slip band over bottom of card.

Sources: Card stock from ANW Crestwood/The Paper Company and Wausau Paper; rubber stamps from Hampton Art and Inkadinkado; Super Fine Detail embossing powder from Ranger Industries Inc.; Versamark watermark ink pad from Tsukineko Inc.; pearl stickers from Michaels Stores Inc.; die templates from Spellbinders Paper Arts; scoring board and tool from Scor-Pal Products; adhesive dots from Glue Dots International.

Table-Number Card

On scoring board, angle 12 x 12-inch piece of silver metallic card stock at 30 degrees. Score lines ½ inch apart, and then change orientation to opposite 30 degrees and score lines in same manner.

From scored card stock, cut one 3¾ x 5¾-inch panel. Trim top corners of scored silver metallic panel to make tag shape. Adhere scored tag shape to white card stock. Trim all around to leave narrow border. Punch hole at top of layered tag.

Using Classic Lace Border Grand Die Template and white card stock, cut and emboss one border. Trim length to 3¾ inches and adhere across width of tag on scored panel, approximately ½ inch from bottom edge.

Materials
- Card stock: white, silver metallic
- "Happily Ever After" rubber stamp
- Silver embossing powder
- Watermark ink pad
- Pearl stickers
- 1¼-inch-wide white silk ribbon
- Small silver brad
- Borderabilities® Classic Lace Border Grand Die Template (#S7-014)
- Nestabilities® Die Templates: Petite Scalloped Ovals Large (#S4-139), Petite Ovals Small (#S4-140)
- Shapeabilities® Die Templates: Flower Creations (#S4-072), Sunflower Set Two (#S4-158), Doodle Parts (#S4-121)
- Manual die-cutting machine
- Embossing heat tool
- ¾-inch circle punch
- Silver teacup holder
- Scoring board and tool
- Transparent tape
- Adhesive foam squares
- Adhesive dots
- Computer and printer (optional)

Hand-print or use computer to generate 1¼-inch-tall table number on white card stock. Using Petite Ovals Small Die Template, cut and emboss one 2¼ x 3⅜-inch oval from printed white card stock, with number centered in oval. Use watermark ink pad to stamp filigree portion of rubber stamp above and below number; emboss with silver embossing powder. Embellish with pearl stickers.

Using Petite Scalloped Ovals Large and silver metallic card stock, cut and emboss one oval slightly larger than white oval. Adhere white oval to silver oval with glue dots. Adhere layered ovals to front of tag with foam squares.

Using Flower Creations, cut and emboss one each eight-petal and small five-petal flowers from white card stock. Cut and emboss one small sunflower using Sunflower Set Two and white card stock. Layer small five-petal and eight-petal flowers with small sunflower to create paper flower. Secure with a small brad through centers. Using an adhesive dot, adhere flower to on lower left corner of tag. Curl and shape flowers to add dimension.

Using Doodle Parts, cut and emboss two of largest swirls from white card stock. Using adhesive dots, adhere ends of swirls behind flower, trimming to fit as needed. Place a pearl sticker on top of brad.

Embellish front of tag card with pearl stickers. Tie a 12-inch length of ribbon through hole in top of tag. Hang tag from teacup holder.

Sources: Card stock from ANW Crestwood/The Paper Company and Wausau Paper; "Happily Ever After" rubber stamp from Hampton Art; Super Fine Detail embossing powder from Ranger Industries Inc.; Versamark watermark ink pad from Tsukineko Inc.; pearl stickers from Michaels Stores Inc.; silk ribbon from May Arts; die templates from Spellbinders Paper Arts; scoring board and tool from Scor-Pal Products; adhesive dots from Glue Dots International.

White Flower Topiary

On scoring board, angle 12 x 12-inch piece of silver metallic card stock at 30 degrees. Score lines ½ inch apart, then change orientation to opposite 30 degrees and score lines in same manner. Cut a 4¾ x 6½-inch panel to cover vase.

On each long edge, punch six holes equally spaced; insert loopy brads in holes. Lace ⅜-inch-wide white satin ribbon through brads and draw up to fit vase.

Insert white dowel into empty ribbon bobbin. Wrap with white tulle and place in vase. Fill vase with tulle.

From white card stock, use Sunflower Set One large flower die template and Flower Creations large five-petal die template to cut multiple flowers.

Fold each sunflower in half and curl petals using scissors. Bring ends together to form a circle and secure with an adhesive dot. Curl petals of five-petal flowers. Layer one sunflower circle with a five-petal flower in center to form flowers. Secure to plastic foam ball with corsage pin through center of each flower. Continue to cover ball.

Curl lengths of silver cord around pencil and tie randomly around heads of corsage pins.

Set plastic foam ball onto dowel and glue for stability.

Tie 1½-inch-wide white satin ribbon in a bow below topiary and at top of vase. Secure bows with adhesive dots.

Sources: Card stock from ANW Crestwood/The Paper Company and Wausau Paper; pearl stickers from Michaels Stores Inc.; satin ribbon from May Arts; Styrofoam brand plastic foam ball from The Dow Chemical Co.; die templates from Spellbinders Paper Arts; scoring board and tool from Scor-Pal Products; Zip Dry Paper Glue from Beacon Adhesives Inc; adhesive dots from Glue Dots International.

Materials
- 7–8-inch-tall glass vase with straight sides
- Card stock: white, silver metallic
- Pearl stickers
- White satin ribbon: 1½-inch-wide, ⅜-inch-wide
- Silver loopy brads
- Silver cord
- White tulle
- Corsage pins
- 16 inches white ⁵/₁₆-inch wooden dowel
- 5-inch plastic foam ball
- Empty 1½-inch-wide ribbon bobbin
- Shapeabilities® Die Templates: Flower Creations (#S4-072), Sunflower Set One (#S4-157)
- Manual die-cutting machine
- ⅛-inch hole punch
- Scoring board and tool
- Instant-dry paper glue
- Adhesive dots

Wedding Gift Tin

On scoring board, angle 12 x 12-inch piece of silver metallic card stock at 30 degrees. Score lines ½ inch apart, and then change orientation to opposite 30 degrees and score lines in same manner. Set aside.

Using Classic Lace Border Grand Die Template, cut and emboss three borders from white card stock. Set two borders aside.

Adhere third border around circumference of tin even with bottom edge. Cut a 1-inch-wide strip from scored silver metallic card stock and adhere around tin over top of lace border. Embellish scored strip and lace border with pearl stickers.

Cut one of the set-aside borders in half; discard one of the halves. Using tape, adhere one end of short border piece to one end of long border piece. Accordian-fold entire length of border. Adhere opposite ends together with tape to form circle.

Using Standard Circles Large Die Template, cut a 2¾-inch circle from silver metallic card stock. Place adhesive dots on back of lace-border circle at north, south, east and west points and attach to silver metallic circle. Use additional adhesive dots as needed to secure. Adhere assembled circle to top of tin lid using foam squares.

Using Standard Circles Large Die Template, cut and emboss a 2⅜-inch circle from white card stock. Stamp filigree portion of rubber stamp on top half of circle with watermark ink pad; emboss with silver embossing powder. Turn circle and repeat on lower half of circle to create a mirror image. Embellish with pearl stickers.

Using Classic Scalloped Circles Small Die Template, cut and emboss a 3-inch circle from silver metallic card stock. Adhere to center top of lace-border circle. Cut a 12-inch length of silk ribbon and loop, placing one leg over the other; secure to top of silver scalloped circle with adhesive dots.

With foam squares, adhere stamped circle over ribbon. Cut and emboss two of the largest swirls from Doodle Parts Die Templates using white card stock. Attach one end of each swirl underneath center round panel with adhesive dots, trimming to fit as needed.

Sources: Card stock from ANW Crestwood/The Paper Company and Wausau Paper; "Happily Ever After" rubber stamp from Hampton Art; Super Fine Detail embossing powder from Ranger Industries Inc.; Versamark watermark ink pad from Tsukineko Inc.; pearl stickers from Michaels Stores Inc.; silk ribbon from May Arts; die templates from Spellbinders Paper Arts; scoring board and tool from Scor-Pal Products; adhesive dots from Glue Dots International.

Materials

- 4¼-inch-diameter x 2¼-inch tall metal tin with lid
- Card stock: white, silver metallic
- "Happily Ever After" rubber stamp
- Silver embossing powder
- Watermark ink pad
- Pearl stickers
- 1¼-inch-wide white silk ribbon
- Borderabilities® Classic Lace Border Grand Die Template (#S7-014)
- Nestabilities® Die Templates: Standard Circles Large Die Template (#S4-114), Classic Scalloped Circles Small Die Template (#S4-125)
- Shapeabilities® Doodle Parts Die Template (#S4-121)
- Manual die-cutting machine
- Embossing heat tool
- Scoring board and tool
- Transparent tape
- Adhesive foam squares
- Adhesive dots

Pretty Pastels

Designs by Linda Duke, courtesy of Spellbinders

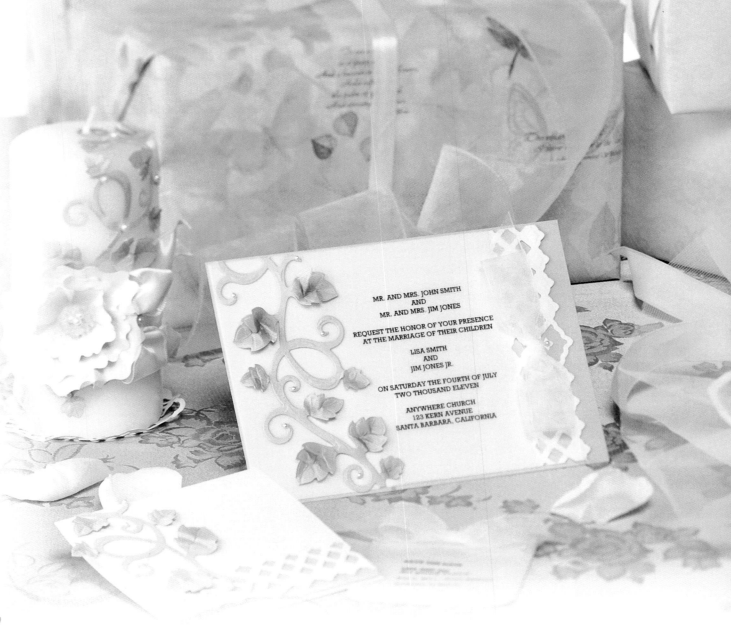

MR. AND MRS. JOHN SMITH
AND
MR. AND MRS. JIM JONES

REQUEST THE HONOR OF YOUR PRESENCE
AT THE MARRIAGE OF THEIR CHILDREN

LISA SMITH
AND
JIM JONES JR.

ON SATURDAY THE FOURTH OF JULY
TWO THOUSAND ELEVEN

ANYWHERE CHURCH
123 KERN AVENUE
SANTA BARBARA, CALIFORNIA

Save-the-Date
Pocket Card

Cut a 10½ x 4½-inch piece from Whisper White card stock. With long side horizontal, score 4⅛ inches and 8½ inches from right edge for card base.

Using Lattice Die Template, cut and emboss right edge of scored card base. Use large scallop punch to create scallop on left edge of card base. Fold card base on scored lines; adhere outer edges of scallop-edge flap to sides of card to make a pocket.

From Blush Blossom card stock, cut one 4½ x 2½-inch piece and one 3 x 3½-inch piece; use On the Vine Border Grand Die Template to cut and emboss one vine. Use marker to tint leaves on vine.

Adhere 4½ x 2½-inch piece of Blush Blossom to bottom of card base behind lattice edge. Trim vine to fit front of card and adhere as shown. Bend leaves to shape. Embellish vine with pearls. Adhere a pearl to center of lattice border.

From Whisper White card stock, cut a 4½ x 4-inch piece. Adhere to inside front of card, covering Blush Blossom card stock. Embellish inside of card with remaining pieces from vine.

Hand-print, or use computer to generate, save-the-date text on vellum. Cut vellum to fit over 3 x 3½-inch Blush Blossom piece and adhere at top edge. Use corner rounders to shape corners.

Tie an 8-inch length of ribbon in a bow. Adhere bow to top of save-the-date message. Slip message inside pocket of card.

Sources: Card stock from Stampin' Up!; self-adhesive pearls from Kaisercraft; Copic markers from Imagination International Inc.; die templates from Spellbinders Paper Arts.

Materials

- **Card stock: Whisper White, Blush Blossom**
- **Vellum**
- **¾-inch-wide white sheer ribbon**
- **White self-adhesive pearls**
- **Willow G24 Copic marker**
- **Airbrush marker system**
- **Borderabilities® Die Templates: Lattice (#S4-218), On the Vine Border Grand (#S7-017)**
- **Large scallop punch**
- **Corner rounder**
- **Manual die-cutting machine**
- **Transparent double-sided tape**
- **Computer and printer (optional)**

SAVE THE DATE
ND JIM
ng hi

Cut a 7 x 5-inch piece of Blush Blossom card stock for base. Using Lattice Die Template, cut and emboss Whisper White card stock and adhere to card base, ¼ inch from right-hand side.

Using On the Vine Border Grand Die Template, cut and emboss vine from Blush Blossom card stock. Cut to fit card front. Use marker to tint leaves on vine. Set aside.

Hand-print, or use computer to generate, invitation text on vellum. Cut vellum 5½ x 4¾ inches. *Note: Place text on right-hand side of vellum to allow placement of vine.* Adhere vellum to card as shown.

Adhere vine to card. Bend leaves to shape. Embellish vine with pearls.

Tie a 12-inch length of ribbon in a bow and adhere to center of lattice border. Adhere a pearl to border next to bow.

Sources: Card stock from Stampin' Up!; self-adhesive pearls from Kaisercraft; Copic markers from Imagination International Inc.; die templates from Spellbinders Paper Arts.

Materials

- **Card stock: Whisper White, Blush Blossom**
- **Vellum**
- **¾-inch-wide white sheer ribbon**
- **White self-adhesive pearls**
- **Willow G24 Copic marker**
- **Airbrush marker system**
- **Borderabilities® Die Templates: Lattice (#S4-218), On the Vine Border Grand (#S7-017)**
- **Manual die-cutting machine**
- **Double-sided transparent adhesive dots**
- **Computer and printer (optional)**

MR. AND MRS. JOHN SMITH
AND
MR. AND MRS. JIM JONES
REQUEST THE HONOR OF YOUR PRESENCE
AT THE MARRIAGE OF THEIR CHILDREN

LISA SMITH
AND
JIM JONES JR.

ON SATURDAY THE FOURTH OF JULY
TWO THOUSAND ELEVEN

ANYWHERE CHURCH
123 KERN AVENUE
SANTA BARBARA, CALIFORNIA

Pretty Bridal Bouquet

Using Peony Die Template and Whisper White card stock, cut and emboss approximately 15 sets of flowers, comprised of three layers each and varying in size. Use fruit pink and barium yellow markers to airbrush flower centers. Press flower sections into palm of your hand to shape. Lightly airbrush edges of some flowers with pale pink.

Apply adhesive to centers of flowers and add ivory sprinkles. Cut a large circle of white tulle and adhere to bottom inside of bridal bouquet handle. Glue plastic foam ball inside bridal bouquet handle. Set all aside to dry.

Using Sunflower Set Two leaf die template, cut and emboss approximately five leaves from card stock. Lightly airbrush with willow marker. Bend to shape. Glue evenly spaced around rim of bridal bouquet holder, leaving space at front for bow.

Assemble flowers, securing with glue. Attach to plastic foam ball using adhesive and pearl-head straight pins through centers of flowers. ***Note:*** *Wait for glue to dry before attaching next flower.*

Wrap handle of bouquet holder with sheer ribbon. Tie wired satin ribbon in a bow and attach to front of bouquet with glue and pins.

Sources: Card stock from Stampin' Up!; Styrofoam brand plastic foam ball from The Dow Chemical Co.; colored sprinkles from Flower Soft Inc.; die templates from Spellbinders Paper Arts; Copic markers and airbrush marker system from Imagination International Inc.; Quick-Grip all-purpose permanent adhesive from Beacon Adhesives Inc.

Materials
- Whisper White card stock
- Ivory-color sprinkles
- White tulle
- White pearl-head straight pins
- White ribbon: ¾-inch-wide wired satin, ¾-inch-wide sheer
- White bridal bouquet handle
- White plastic foam ball to fit bouquet handle
- Copic markers: barium yellow Y00, fruit pink E02, pale pink RV10, willow G24
- Airbrush marker system
- Nestabilities® Peony Die Templates (#S4-193)
- Shapeabilities® Sunflower Set Two Die Templates (#S4-158)
- Manual die-cutting machine
- All-purpose permanent adhesive

Wedding Candle

Project note: *Candle is for decoration only; do not burn with paper decorations.*

Using On the Vine Border Grand Die Template and Blush Blossom card stock, cut and emboss one vine. Tint leaves using willow marker. Apply vine to candle with straight pins and heat-set in place with heat gun. Bend leaves to shape.

Using Peony No. 1, No. 2 and No. 3 Die Templates, cut and emboss one of each petal from Whisper White card stock. Tint with pale pink, barium yellow, rose pink and fruit pink markers. Press flowers in palm of hand to shape. Assemble flowers, securing with glue.

Make a slight indentation in candle for placement of flower. Tie a length of ribbon in a bow around candle, covering indentation; secure with straight pin through knot and heat set with heat gun.

Attach flower to candle with four straight pins through center of flower.

Using Lattice Pendants Die Template, cut one pendant from Whisper White card stock. Adhere to bottom of candle.

Sources: Card stock from Stampin' Up!; colored sprinkles from Flower Soft Inc.; Copic markers from Imagination International Inc.; die templates from Spellbinders Paper Arts.

Materials
- 6-inch-tall pillar candle
- Card stock: Whisper White, Blush Blossom
- Ivory-color sprinkles
- ¾-inch-wide wired white satin ribbon
- White pearl-head straight pins
- Copic markers: pale pink RV10, barium yellow Y00, rose pink S-R81, fruit pink E02, willow G24
- Airbrush marker system
- Borderabilities® On the Vine Border Grand Die Template (#S7-017)
- Shapeabilities® Lattice Pendants Die Template (#S4-210)
- Nestabilities® Peony Die Templates (#S4-193)
- Manual die-cutting machine
- Craft heat gun
- Paper adhesive

Materials

- Card stock: Whisper White, Blush Blossom
- Ivory-color sprinkles
- ⅜-inch-wide white satin ribbon
- White self-adhesive pearls
- Copic markers: pale pink RV10, barium yellow Y00, rose pink S-R81, fruit pink E02, willow G24
- Airbrush marker system
- Mega-Nestabilities® Curved Rectangles Die Templates (#S5-006)
- Borderabilities® Die Templates: Lattice (#S4-218), On the Vine Border Grand (#S7-017)
- Nestabilities® Peony Die Template (#S4-193)
- Manual die-cutting machine
- Paper adhesive

Thank You Card

Form 3¾ x 5½-inch top-fold card from Whisper White card stock for card base.

Using Curved Rectangles No. 6 Die Template, cut and emboss rectangle from Whisper White card stock. Use Lattice Die Template to cut border on one short edge of white curved rectangle. Adhere to Blush Blossom card stock and trim to create narrow border, cutting straight across lattice edge.

Using On the Vine Border Grand Die Template and Blush Blossom card stock, cut and emboss one vine. Tint leaves using willow marker. Bend leaves to shape. Position and adhere vine to solid portion of white rectangle, trimming to fit as needed.

Using Peony No. 1 and No. 2 Die Templates, cut two flowers from Whisper White card stock. Tint with pale pink, barium yellow, rose pink and fruit pink markers. Press flowers in palm of hand to shape, and then adhere together. Apply adhesive to center of flower and add ivory sprinkles. Adhere flower to vine.

Embellish vine, flower center and lattice border with pearls. Tie a 14-inch length of ribbon around card front. Adhere card front to front of card base.

Sources: Card stock from Stampin' Up!; self-adhesive pearls from Kaisercraft; colored sprinkles from Flower Soft Inc.; Copic markers from Imagination International Inc.; die templates from Spellbinders Paper Arts.

Trim ¼ inch from two adjacent sides of one 12 x 12-inch sheet of Whisper White card stock. Center and adhere to 12 x 12-inch sheet of Blush Blossom card stock.

In the center of an 8½ x 11-inch sheet of Whisper White card stock, cut a curved rectangle using Curved Rectangles No. 6 Die Template. Sponge ink pad around center cut-out edges to shade. Place over photo with image centered. Adhere both to large layered card stock squares.

Hand-print or use computer to generate the word "Cherish" on Whisper White card stock. Using Long Classic Rectangles Large No. 3 Die Template, cut and emboss a rectangle from printed card stock. Use peach ink pad to shade edges. Adhere above photo.

Using On the Vine Border Grand Die Template, cut and emboss vines from Blush Blossom card stock. Tint leaves using willow marker. Bend leaves to shape. Adhere vines around photo, piecing as needed to create a rounded shape.

Using Peony Die Templates and white card stock, cut and emboss one complete set of flowers and one flower each using only No. 1 and No. 2 Die Templates. Tint with pale pink, barium yellow, rose pink and fruit pink markers. Press flowers in palm of hand to shape. Assemble flowers and secure with adhesive. Apply adhesive to center of each flower and add sprinkles. Adhere flowers below photo.

Embellish vines and flowers with pearls. Tie a 36-inch length of ribbon around bottom of card stock below flowers.

Sources: Card stock from Stampin' Up!; colored sprinkles from Flower Soft Inc.; self-adhesive pearls from Kaisercraft; Copic markers from Imagination International Inc.; die templates from Spellbinders Paper Arts.

Materials
- **Card stock: Whisper White, Blush Blossom**
- **Ivory-color sprinkles**
- **¾-inch-wide wired white satin ribbon**
- **White self-adhesive pearls**
- **Copic markers: pale pink RV10, barium yellow Y00, rose pink S-R81, fruit pink E02, willow G24**
- **Peach ink pad**
- **Borderabilities® On the Vine Border Grand Die Template (#S7-017)**
- **Nestabilities® Die Templates: Long Classic Rectangles Large (#S4-142), Peony (#S4-193)**
- **Mega-Nestabilities® Curved Rectangles Die Templates (#S5-006)**
- **Manual die-cutting machine**
- **Paper adhesive**
- **Computer and printer (optional)**

Red Radiance

Designs by Jennifer Davis, courtesy of Spellbinders

Invitation

Form a 5 x 7-inch side-folded card from red card stock for card base.

Cut a 4¾ x 6¾-inch piece from white card stock. Using repositionable adhesive, attach to front of card base. Using Labels Eight No. 3 Die Template, cut a window in front of card through both layers, positioning it in upper right-hand portion of card. Remove white card stock.

To add color and pattern to front of white card stock, remove Flowers Embellishment Template from its outside frame. Apply a layer of red ink directly onto Flowers and Labels Eight No. 3 Die Templates.

Place Labels Eight No. 3 Die Template into window previously cut in white card stock. Place Flowers Embellishment Template horizontally along top of front side of white card stock, leaving No. 3 Die Template in place. Emboss with die-cutting machine. Repeat process with bottom half of white card stock.

Permanently attach printed white card stock to front of card, realigning windows.

Using On the Vine Border Grand Die Template, cut one vine from light blue card stock. Stencil through back of die using clear ink, and then emboss with clear embossing powder. Curl leaves by wrapping around a pencil.

Materials

- **Card stock: red, lilac, white, light blue**
- **Photo paper (optional)**
- **Clear embossing powder**
- **Ink pads: clear, red**
- **Self-adhesive pearls**
- **Small multicolored acrylic stones**
- **Shapeabilities® Die Templates: Floral Accent (#S4-199), Kaleidoscope Pendants (#S4-207)**
- **Impressabilities™ Flowers Embellishment Templates (#I2-1004)**
- **Borderabililties® On the Vine Border Grand Die Template (#S7-017)**
- **Nestabilities® Labels Eight Die Template (#S5-019)**
- **Manual die-cutting machine**
- **Embossing heat tool**
- **Tweezers**
- **Adhesive foam squares**
- **Adhesive dots**
- **Repositionable adhesive**
- **Paper adhesive**
- **Computer with printer (optional)**

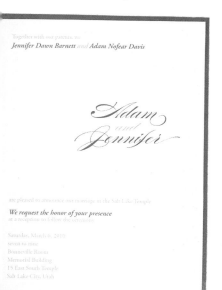

Use Kaleidoscope Pendants center die template to cut shape from red card stock. Emboss with clear ink and embossing powder as for vine. Adhere pearls to pendant center.

Using Floral Accent Die Templates and lilac card stock, cut and emboss one set. Using smallest die template from Floral Accent, cut three from red card stock.

Cut vine into pieces and arrange on front of card with floral accents, using foam squares for dimension. Adhere pendant center over vine and floral accents in lower left portion of card.

Use tweezers and paper adhesive to accent card front with acrylic stones.

Hand-print on card stock, or use computer to generate on photo paper, the invitation text, positioning names of bride and groom so they will be visible through the card window. Trim to fit and attach inside card.

Sources: Card stock from WorldWin Papers, Neenah Paper Inc. and My Mind's Eye; embossing powder from Stampendous! Inc.; ink pads from Tsukineko Inc.; Bits of Bling pearls from Creative Impressions Inc.; Tiny Twinkles from Taylored Expressions; die templates from Spellbinders Paper Arts; adhesive dots from Glue Dots International.

RSVP Card

Cut red card stock to 5½ x 4¼ inches for card base.

Hand-print text on white card stock, or use computer to generate text on photo paper. Trim to 5¼ x 4 inches. Adhere to card base.

Apply a layer of red ink onto Flowers Embellishment Templates; place onto 4 x 1-inch strip of white card stock and emboss with die-cutting machine. Adhere strip to red card stock and trim to make a border. Cut layered strip into two unequal sections. Fold sections over edges of card on left and right sides; attach with adhesive.

Using On the Vine Border Grand Die Template and light blue card stock, cut and emboss one vine. Stencil through back of die with clear ink, and then emboss with clear embossing powder. Curl leaves by wrapping around a pencil. Cut vine into smaller sections.

Using Floral Accent Die Templates and red card stock, cut and emboss one set. Arrange vine sections and floral accents on card front using foam squares to add dimension.

Remove two beaded stems from spray. Twist wire stems together and attach to front of card with glue dots. Embellish card with pearls.

Sources: Card stock from WorldWin Papers, Neenah Paper Inc. and My Mind's Eye; embossing powder from Stampendous! Inc.; ink pads from Tsukineko Inc.; Bits of Bling pearls from Creative Impressions Inc.; Tiny Twinkles from Taylored Expressions; die templates from Spellbinders Paper Arts.

Materials
- **Card stock: red, white, light blue**
- **Photo paper (optional)**
- **Clear embossing powder**
- **Ink pads: clear, red**
- **Self-adhesive pearls**
- **Red faceted beaded spray**
- **Shapeabilities® Floral Accent Die Templates (#S4-199)**
- **Impressabilities™ Flowers Embellishment Templates (#I2-1004)**
- **Borderabililties® On the Vine Border Grand Die Template (#S7-017)**
- **Manual die-cutting machine**
- **Embossing heat tool**
- **Foam squares**
- **Glue dots**
- **Paper adhesive**
- **Computer with printer (optional)**

Keepsake Box

Paint outside of box and lid with acrylic paint, applying multiple coats as needed to cover. Line inside of box with red card stock.

Hand-print on white card stock, or use a computer to generate on photo paper, title for box, sizing it to fit inside Labels Eight No. 5 Die Template.

Apply red ink to Labels Eight No. 5 die template, then cut and emboss title paper.

Cut a 5½ x 2-inch strip from white card stock. Apply a layer of red ink directly onto Flowers Embellishment Templates to emboss strip.

Cut strip into two sections. Adhere each section onto red card stock and trim to form a small border. Adhere strips to top of box lid, folding edges over ends of lid. Adhere title label to top of box over gap between embossed strips.

Using On the Vine Border Grand Die Template and light blue card stock, cut and emboss one vine. Stencil through back of template with clear ink and emboss with clear embossing powder. Curl leaves by wrapping around a pencil.

Using Kaleidoscope Pendants Die Template, cut and emboss three pendant centers from red card stock. Stencil and emboss as for vine. Attach pearls to centers of pendant centers.

Using Floral Accent Die Templates and lilac card stock, cut and emboss one set.

Cut vine into smaller sections and arrange on box lid with floral accents and pendant centers, using foam squares to add dimension.

Sources: Card stock from WorldWin Papers, Neenah Paper Inc. and My Mind's Eye; embossing powder from Stampendous! Inc.; ink pads from Tsukineko Inc.; Bits of Bling pearls from Creative Impressions Inc.; die templates from Spellbinders Paper Arts; adhesive dots from Glue Dots International.

Materials
- 8½ x 4 x 6½-inch papier-mâché box with lid and embossed border
- Card stock: red, lilac, white, light blue
- Photo paper (optional)
- Clear embossing powder
- Ink pads: clear, red
- Self-adhesive pearls
- Light blue acrylic paint
- Shapeabilities® Die Templates: Floral Accent (#S4-199), Kaleidoscope Pendants (#S4-207)
- Impressabilities™
- Flowers Embellishment Template (#I2-1004)
- Borderabililties® On the Vine Border Grand Die Template (#S7-017)
- Nestabilities® Labels Eight Die Template (#S5-019)
- Manual die-cutting machine
- Embossing heat tool
- Paintbrush
- Tweezers
- Adhesive foam squares
- Adhesive dots
- Paper adhesive
- Computer with printer (optional)

Thank You Card

Form a 6 x 6-inch side-folded card from red card stock for card base.

Using Labels Eight No. 6 Die Template, cut folded card base so that folded edge stays just inside cut blade of die. ***Note:*** *Use repositionable adhesive if needed.*

Score front of card at halfway point and fold forward to create a Z shape.

Apply a layer of red ink directly onto Flowers Embellishment Templates and Labels Eight No. 4 Die Templates. Cut a label from white card stock using inked No. 4 Die Template, and then place inked Flowers Embellishment Templates under the No. 4 die and card stock when embossing to complete letter-press effect.

Using On the Vine Border Grand Die Template and light blue card stock, cut and emboss two vines. Stencil through back of die template using clear ink and then emboss with clear embossing powder. Open card and lay flat. Adhere one vine across entire width of card, scoring in the middle so vine bends with card.

Close card and adhere letter-press label, centering it on fold.

Using Kaleidoscope Pendants Die Template and red card stock, cut and emboss one pendant center. Stencil and emboss as for vine. Adhere pearls in the center.

Using Floral Accent Die Template and lilac card stock, cut and emboss one set of accents.

Wrap leaves on remaining vine around a pencil to curl. Cut vine into several pieces and arrange with floral accents and pendant center on front label, using foam squares to add dimension.

Apply red ink to Labels Eight No. 2 Die Template, cut and emboss label from white card stock. Use stamp and red ink to stamp "thank you ever so much" on label. Adhere label to inside of card with foam square.

Sources: Card stock from WorldWin Papers, Neenah Paper Inc. and My Mind's Eye; stamp from Hero Arts; embossing powder from Stampendous! Inc.; ink pads from Tsukineko Inc.; Bits of Bling pearls from Creative Impressions Inc.; die templates from Spellbinders Paper Arts.

Materials
- Card stock: red, lilac, white, light blue
- Clear Design Thoughtful Messages stamp (#CL184)
- Clear embossing powder
- Ink pads: clear, red
- Self-adhesive pearls
- Shapeabilities® Die Templates: Floral Accent (#S4-199), Kaleidoscope Pendants (#S4-207)
- Impressabilities™ Flowers Embellishment Template (#I2-1004)
- Borderabililties® On the Vine Border Grand Die Template (#S7-017)
- Nestabilities® Labels Eight Die Template (#S5-019)
- Manual die-cutting machine
- Embossing heat tool
- Foam squares
- Glue dots
- Repositionable adhesive (optional)

Bliss
We were married on a beautiful, crisp spring morning in Salt Lake City. The ceremony was beautiful and I am so happy to be partners with such a wonderful man. I'm looking forward to the rest of our lives together.
We had an elegant luncheon at the Inn at Temple Square and later in the evening we gathered for a reception in the beautiful Joseph Smith Memorial Building.
Friends and family attended from all over the country and it was such a blessing to have everyone with us at the beginning of our journey together.

Scrapbook Page

Apply a layer of red ink directly onto Flowers Embellishment Templates. Emboss three pieces of white card stock, re-inking between each piece.

Cut each piece into 1-inch-wide strips. Adhere strips around edge of a 12 x 12-inch piece of red card stock.

Adhere 4 x 12-inch photo print to right side of layout. Apply strips of blue decorative tape to edge of layout and sides of photo.

Using On the Vine Border Grand Die Template and light blue card stock, cut and emboss two vines. Stencil from back of die template using clear ink, and then emboss with clear embossing powder. Curl leaves by wrapping around a pencil.

Using Kaleidoscope Pendants Die Template, cut and emboss four pendant centers from red card stock. Stencil and emboss as for vine. Attach pearls to centers of pendant centers.

Using Floral Accent Die Templates and lilac card stock, cut and emboss one set of accents.

Cut vine into several long pieces and arrange on left side of layout with floral accents and pendant centers, using foam squares to add dimension. Arrange another set of accents on bottom right corner of layout.

Hand-print on white card stock, or use computer to generate on photo paper, journaling, sizing to fit inside Label Eight No. 5 Die Template. Apply red ink to die template, and then cut and emboss journaling paper. Adhere journaling to lower right portion of layout.

Use computer to generate the title, and then flip the text so mirror image shows. Create a shadow of the title as well, and flip it. Print title onto red, light blue and white card stock. Use a craft knife to cut along printed lines of the title. For blue piece, do not cut out centers of letters. Turn titles to the right side and adhere them together: red onto blue onto white. Adhere to layout.

Sources: Card stock from WorldWin Papers, Neenah Paper Inc. and My Mind's Eye; embossing powder from Stampendous! Inc.; ink pads from Tsukineko Inc.; Bits of Bling pearls from Creative Impressions Inc.; Tiny Twinkles from Taylored Expressions; die templates from Spellbinders Paper Arts; blue decorative tape from Heidi Swapp/Advantus Corp.; adhesive dots from Glue Dots International.

Materials
- **Card stock: red, lilac, white, light blue**
- **Photo paper (optional)**
- **4 x 12-inch photo print**
- **Clear embossing powder**
- **Ink pads: clear, red**
- **Self-adhesive pearls**
- **Small multicolored acrylic stones**
- **Shapeabilities® Die Templates: Floral Accent (#S4-199), Kaleidoscope Pendants (#S4-207)**
- **Impressabilities™ Flowers Embellishment Templates (#I2-1004)**
- **Borderabililties® On the Vine Border Grand Die Template (#S7-017)**
- **Nestabilities® Labels Eight Die Templates (#S5-019)**
- **Manual die-cutting machine**
- **Embossing heat tool**
- **Tweezers**
- **Blue decorative tape**
- **Foam squares**
- **Glue dots**
- **Computer with printer**

Ornament

Apply red alcohol ink to surface of ornament with a scrap of felt. Let dry.

Materials
- **Clear frosted-glass ornament**
- **Light blue card stock**
- **Scrap of felt**
- **Clear embossing powder**
- **Clear ink pad**
- **Red alcohol ink**
- **Self-adhesive pearls**
- **Light blue cord**
- **Borderabililties® On the Vine Border Grand Die Template (#S7-017)**
- **Manual die-cutting machine**
- **Sticker-making machine**
- **Embossing heat tool**
- **Craft adhesive**

Using On the Vine Border Grand Die Template and light blue card stock, cut and emboss one vine. Stencil through back of die template with clear ink and emboss with clear embossing powder. Run vine through sticker-making machine to apply adhesive to back. Adhere vine to ornament.

Embellish ornament with pearls.

Wrap and glue a long piece of blue cord around top of ornament, tying it to top ring and creating a large hanging loop.

Sources: Card stock from My Mind's Eye; embossing powder from Stampendous! Inc.; ink pad from Tsukineko Inc.; alcohol ink from Ranger Industries Inc.; Bits of Bling pearls from Creative Impressions Inc.; die templates from Spellbinders Paper Arts.

Earth Tones Suite

Designs by Kimberly Crawford, courtesy of Spellbinders

Thank You

The favor of a reply is requested
by July 21, 2010.

M _____

____ Accepts with pleasure
____ Declines with regret.

With joyful hearts, we ask you to
be present at the ceremony uniting

Kimberly Kae Allen

And

Gregory Ethan John

Saturday, the fourteenth of
August,
two thousand and ten
at 7 o'clock in the evening
Moose Lake Church
Moose Lake, Minnesota

Invitation

Cut a 4 x 9¼-inch rectangle from green card stock for card base.

Cut a 3⅞ x 9-inch rectangle from antique white card stock. Hand-print, or use computer to generate, invitation text on upper portion of rectangle for card front.

Using Flowers Embellishment Templates, emboss silver vellum. Cut a 3⅞ x 2½-inch piece; adhere to antique white rectangle below text.

Cut a length of ribbon the width of the card and adhere to vellum.

Using Tags Five square Die Template, cut and emboss one tag from antique white card stock. Stamp tag with "Two Hearts One Love."

Thread tag onto cream button twine and tie around card front so it lies over ribbon. Secure tag with a small bit of adhesive.

Adhere card front to card base.

Sources: Card stock from Bazzill Basics Paper Inc. and Papertrey Ink; vellum from ANW Crestwood/The Paper Company; stamp, ink pad and button twine from Papertrey Ink; die templates from Spellbinders Paper Arts.

Materials
- **Card stock: green, antique white**
- **Silver vellum**
- **"Two Hearts One Love" stamp**
- **Brown ink pad**
- **1³⁄₁₆-inch-wide green picot-edge satin ribbon**
- **Cream button twine**
- **Shapeabilities® Tags Five Die Templates (#S4-081)**
- **Impressabilities™ Flowers Embellishment Templates (#I2-1004)**
- **Paper adhesive**
- **Computer and printer (optional)**

RSVP Card

Using Labels Eight No. 6 Die Template, cut and emboss one label from green card stock.

Hand-print, or use computer to generate, text on antique white card stock. Using Labels Eight No. 5 Die Template, cut one label from printed text card stock, keeping wording centered and even. Emboss label using Flowers Embellishment Templates.

The favor of a reply is requested by July 21, 2010.

*M*_____

____ *Accepts with pleasure*
____ *Declines with regrets*

Materials
- **Card stock: green, antique white**
- **Nestabilities® Labels Eight Die Templates (#S5-019)**
- **Impressabilities™ Flowers Embellishment Templates (#I2-1004)**
- **Manual die-cutting machine**
- **Paper adhesive**
- **Computer and printer (optional)**

Adhere printed and embossed card stock to green label.

Sources: Card stock from Bazzill Basics Paper Inc. and Papertrey Ink; die templates from Spellbinders Paper Arts.

Potpourri Bag

Cut burlap to 4 x 9 inches. Fold one end up, leaving 1½ inches at top for a flap.

Glue two sides together; let dry. Turn bag right side out, pushing corners out. Apply seam sealant to edges of flap to prevent fraying.

Fold flap down and use craft punch to punch two holes through all three thicknesses, centered on flap and spaced approximately ¾ inch apart.

Pull ends of a 14-inch length of ribbon through punched holes. Fill bag with potpourri, and then pull ribbon to draw opening closed; tie in a bow.

Source: Craft Bond Fabric & Paper Glue from Elmer's Products Inc.

Materials
- **Burlap fabric**
- **1³/16-inch-wide green picot-edge satin ribbon**
- **Potpourri**
- **Craft punch**
- **Seam sealant**
- **Fabric adhesive**

Centerpiece

Line inner sides of tray with green card stock.

Cut bamboo canes to cover the outer sides and inner bottom of tray; glue in place.

Using Flowers Embellishment Templates, emboss vellum. Cut vellum to fit around votives. Wrap around votives, overlapping ends slightly. Glue ends to secure.

Adhere a length of ribbon to vellum around each votive.

Using Tags Five square Die Template, cut and emboss one tag from antique white card stock. Stamp "Happily Ever After" with brown ink on tag. Tie tag around a votive with twine.

Arrange votives in tray.

Sources: Card stock from Bazzill Basics Paper Inc. and Papertrey Ink; vellum from ANW Crestwood/The Paper Company; stamp and ink pad from Papertrey Ink; Craft Bond Tacky Glue from Elmer's Products Inc.; die templates from Spellbinders Paper Arts.

Materials
- **Glass votives with candles**
- **Shallow rectangular tin tray**
- **Card stock: green, antique white**
- **Vellum**
- **"Happily Ever After" stamp**
- **Brown ink pad**
- **1³⁄₁₆-inch-wide green picot-edge satin ribbon**
- **Twine**
- **Thin bamboo canes**
- **Shapeabilities® Tags Five Die Template (#S4-081)**
- **Impressabilities™ Flowers Embellishment Templates (#I2-1004)**
- **Manual die-cutting machine**
- **Craft glue**

Materials
- Card stock: kraft, green, antique white
- Silver vellum
- "Thank You" stamp
- Brown ink pad
- 1³⁄16-inch-wide green picot-edge satin ribbon
- Cream button twine
- Shapeabilities® Tags Five Die Template (#S4-081)
- Impressabilities™ Flowers Embellishment Templates (#I2-1004)
- Manual die-cutting machine
- Paper adhesive

Thank You Card

Form a 4¼ x 4¼-inch top-folded card from kraft card stock for card base. Cut a 4 x 4-inch square from green card stock; adhere to front of card base.

Cut a 4¼ x 2-inch strip from silver vellum; emboss using Flowers Embellishment Templates. Adhere to lower half of card front.

Cut a length of ribbon the width of the card and adhere to vellum.

Using Tags Five square Die Template, cut and emboss one tag from antique white card stock. Stamp tag with "Thank You" using brown ink.

Thread tag onto cream button twine and tie around front of card.

Sources: Card stock from Bazzill Basics Paper Inc. and Papertrey Ink; vellum from ANW Crestwood/The Paper Company; stamp, ink pad and button twine from Papertrey Ink; die templates from Spellbinders Paper Arts.

Something Blue

Designs by Karen Taylor, courtesy of Spellbinders

thanks

Save the Date

Save-the-Date Tag

Using Classic Scalloped Rectangles Large No. 5 Die Template and printed paper, cut and emboss four large rectangles. With wrong sides together, adhere together in pairs.

Cut two 2¾ x 7½-inch pieces from dark blue card stock; ink edges dark blue. Sandwich scalloped rectangles (side by side with short edges touching) between dark blue rectangles to form bookmark/tag.

From printed paper, cut two 2½ x 7¼-inch rectangles. Ink edges dark blue and adhere to front and back of tag.

Using Labels Nine Die Templates, cut one No. 4 label from yellow card stock and one No. 5 label from dark blue card stock. Stamp "Save the Date" with dark blue ink in center of yellow label.

Adhere yellow label to dark blue label with foam squares, then adhere dark blue label to tag with foam squares.

Using On the Vine Border Grand Die Template, cut and emboss one vine from green card stock. Ink edges of leaves brown. Fold leaves to add dimension. Cut sections from vine and adhere to front of tag as shown.

Materials
- **Card stock: yellow, green, dark blue**
- **Coordinating printed paper**
- **"Save the Date" stamp**
- **Ink pads: dark blue, brown**
- **⅞-inch-wide sheer dark blue ribbon**
- **Blue ¼-inch eyelet**
- **Shapeabilities® Flower Creations Three Die Templates (#S4-109)**
- **Borderabilities® On the Vine Border Grand Die Template (#S7-017)**
- **Nestabilities® Die Templates: Classic Scalloped Rectangles Large (#S4-133), Labels Nine (#S4-233)**
- **Manual die-cutting machine**
- **Adhesive foam squares**
- **Fast-drying paper adhesive**
- **Floral wire**
- **Wire cutters**
- **Needle-nose pliers**
- **Eyelet-setting tool**

Using Flower Creations Three Die Templates and yellow card stock, cut and emboss three No. 1 flowers, two No. 2 flowers and one No. 3 flower. Ink edges dark blue. Bend to shape.

For large flower, layer No. 1, No. 2 and No. 3 flowers. Pierce two holes in center. Insert a length of floral wire up through hole and back down, twisting end around stem to secure. For medium flower, layer No. 1 and No. 2 flowers. Pierce in center and attach floral wire. Adhere flowers to vine as shown.

Following manufacturer's instructions, attach eyelet at center top of tag. Attach a length of ribbon through eyelet.

Sources: Card stock from Bazzill Basics Paper Inc.; printed paper from BasicGrey; Colorbox ink pads from Clearsnap Inc.; stamp from JustRite Stampers; die templates from Spellbinders Paper Arts.

Invitation

Card

Using Classic Scalloped Rectangle Large No. 5 Die Template, cut and emboss four rectangles from printed paper. With wrong sides together, adhere together in pairs.

Cut two 6 x 3¼-inch rectangles from dark blue card stock. Set one aside. Adhere scalloped rectangles (long edges touching) to wrong side of one dark blue rectangle so scallops on printed-paper rectangles are visible.

Cut a 5½ x 3-inch piece of yellow card stock; adhere to center of dark blue rectangle. Cut a 5 x 2½-inch rectangle from printed paper; ink edges dark blue. Adhere to center of yellow card stock rectangle.

Using Fancy Tags No. 2 Die Template and yellow card stock, cut two tags. Set one aside. Adhere one tag to front of card. Stamp "Our Wedding" on tag with dark blue ink.

Adhere remaining 6 x 3¼-inch dark blue rectangle to back of card on side and bottom edges only. Embellish front of card with a pearl.

Slider

Cut a 5 x 3¼-inch rectangle from yellow card stock. Layer with a 4¾ x 3-inch rectangle of dark blue card stock.

Hand-print, or use a computer to generate, invitation text; cut out to 4¼ x 2¾ inches. Adhere to front of slider.

Fold remaining tag in half and glue together. Adhere to back of slider at center top edge. Embellish with a pearl. Insert slider in card.

Sources: Card stock from Bazzill Basics Paper Inc.; printed paper from BasicGrey; self-adhesive pearls from Kaisercraft; die templates from Spellbinders Paper Arts.

Materials
- **Card stock: yellow, dark blue**
- **Coordinating printed paper**
- **Computer paper**
- **"Our Wedding" stamp**
- **Blue ink pad**
- **Self-adhesive pearls**
- **Shapeabilities® Fancy Tags Die Templates (#S4-235)**
- **Nestabilities® Classic Scalloped Rectangle Large Die Templates (#S4-133)**
- **Manual die-cutting machine**
- **Glue dots**
- **Computer with printer (optional)**

As the night becomes day
Join us as we become one.

McKenna Mae Sparkman
and
Phillip Guy Mills
invite you
to a sunrise celebration of their love.
November twenty second two thousand and eleven
at six am

Breakfast to follow

Materials

- 3 x 1½ x 3-inch papier-mâché box with lid
- Card stock: yellow, green, dark blue
- Coordinating printed paper
- Ink pads: dark blue, yellow, brown
- Tiny pompoms
- Shapeabilities® Flower Creations Three Die Templates (#S4-109)
- Nestabilities® Classic Scalloped Squares Small Die Templates (#S4-129)
- Borderabilities® Die Templates: On the Vine Border Grand (#S7-017), Classic Lace Border Grand (#S7-014)
- Manual die-cutting machine
- Small yellow brad
- Fast-drying paper adhesive
- Computer with printer (optional)

Candy Box

Cover sides of box, and sides and top of lid with printed paper. Ink exposed edges with dark blue.

Using Classic Scalloped Squares Small No. 4 Die Template and yellow card stock, cut and emboss one square. Ink edges yellow. Adhere to top of lid.

Using Classic Lace Border Grand Die Template and dark blue card stock, cut one border. Adhere around sides of box.

Using On the Vine Border Grand Die Templates and green card stock, cut and emboss one vine. Ink edges of leaves brown. Fold leaves upward to shape. Adhere vine to top of lid, trimming to fit.

Using Flower Creations Three Die Templates and printed paper, cut and emboss one ⅞-inch nine-petal flower and three ⅜-inch nine-petal flowers.

Adhere one smaller flower inside larger flower, then adhere layered flowers to top of lid. Adhere remaining two smaller flowers to vine. Ink pompoms with yellow; adhere one pompom in center of each flower.

Sources: Card stock from Bazzill Basics Paper Inc.; printed paper from BasicGrey; Colorbox ink pads from Clearsnap Inc.; die templates from Spellbinders Paper Arts.

Floral Chair Accent

Using Dahlia No. 6 Die Template and dark blue card stock, cut and emboss one dahlia. Ink edges yellow. Fold in fourths and then turn over and do the same to give dimension. With No. 4 Die Template, cut and emboss two more dahlias from dark blue card stock; ink edges and fold as before.

Using Classic Scalloped Heart Die Template and printed paper, die-cut and emboss four 2¼-inch-long hearts and four 1¼-inch-long hearts for large flower; die-cut and emboss four ¾-inch-long hearts for each smaller dahlia. Ink edges yellow.

Adhere four largest hearts behind large dahlia. Crease each of the smaller hearts in center and curl edges over a pencil. Adhere to insides of dahlias.

Pierce two holes in center of each flower. Insert a length of floral wire up through hole and back down, twisting end around stem to secure. Ink stem wire green.

Using Standard Circle Small No. 3 Die Template, cut two circles from yellow card stock. Layer circles and fringe edges to center. Adhere in center of large dahlia. Cut four No. 2 circles; layer in pairs and secure with small brads. Fringe edges to centers. Adhere to centers of smaller dahlias.

Using Flower Creations Three Die Templates and yellow card stock, cut four 1¼-inch nine-petal flowers. Ink edges dark blue. For each flower, cut two more flowers in descending size to make a total of four flowers with three layers each. Pierce centers and attach floral wire as for dahlias. Ink stem wire green.

Using Flower Creations Three Die Templates, cut 10 to 12 large and medium leaves from green card stock. Ink edges brown. Fold each leaf in half to add dimension. Pinch bottom of each leaf and wrap with a length of floral wire. Add adhesive to secure. Ink stem wire green.

Arrange flowers and leaves as shown and wrap stem wires together to secure.

Adhere pompom to center of large dahlia. Tie a bow from sheer dark blue ribbon and attach to back of floral arrangement.

Sources: Card stock from Bazzill Basics Paper Inc.; printed paper from BasicGrey; Colorbox ink pads from Clearsnap Inc.; ribbon from Offray; die templates from Spellbinders Paper Arts.

Materials

- **Card stock: yellow, green, dark blue**
- **Coordinating printed paper**
- **Ink pads: dark blue, yellow, green, brown**
- **Small pompom**
- **Small yellow brads**
- **White floral wire**
- **⅞-inch-wide sheer dark blue ribbon**
- **Shapeabilities® Flower Creations Three Die Templates (#S4-109)**
- **Nestabilities® Die Templates: Dahlia (#S4-191), Classic Scalloped Heart (#S4-137), Standard Circle Small (#S4-116)**
- **Manual die-cutting machine**
- **Fast-drying paper adhesive**

Thank You Card

Form a 6 x 5-inch top-folded card from dark blue card stock for card base.

Cut a piece of yellow card stock to 5¾ x 4¾ inches; ink edges yellow. Adhere to center front of base card.

Cut a piece of printed paper 5½ x 4½ inches; ink edges blue. Adhere to center front of card.

Using On the Vine Border Grand Die Template and green card stock, die-cut and emboss one vine. Ink edges of leaves brown. Fold leaves upward to shape. Adhere vine across front of card, trimming to fit.

Using Dahlia No. 3 Die Template and dark blue card stock, cut one dahlia. Fold in fourths; turn over and fold in fourths again to give dimension.

Using Classic Scalloped Hearts No. 1 Die Template and printed paper, cut four hearts. Adhere hearts to dahlia.

Using Standard Circles Small No. 2 Die Template and yellow card stock, cut two circles. Holding circles together, cut with scissors to fringe edges. Place circles in center of dahlia and secure with brad. Adhere flower to vine.

Using Fancy Tags No. 1 Die Template and yellow card stock, cut and emboss one tag. Stamp "thanks" on tag with blue ink. Adhere tag to card as shown.

Sources: Card stock from Bazzill Basics Paper Inc.; printed paper from BasicGrey; self-adhesive pearls from Kaisercraft; die templates from Spellbinders Paper Arts.

Materials

- Card stock: yellow, green, dark blue
- Coordinating printed paper
- "thanks" stamp
- Small yellow brad
- Ink pads: blue, yellow, brown
- Shapeabilities® Fancy Tags Die Templates (#S4-235)
- Borderabilities® On the Vine Border Grand Die Template (#S7-017)
- Nestabilities® Die Templates: Classic Scalloped Hearts (#S4-137), Standard Circles Small (#S4-116), Dahlia (#S4-191)
- Manual die-cutting machine
- Fast-drying paper adhesive
- Computer with printer (optional)

Buyer's Guide

Projects in this book were made using products provided by the manufacturers listed below. Look for the suggested products in your local craft- and art-supply stores. If unavailable, contact suppliers below. Some may be able to sell products directly to you; others may be able to refer you to retail sources.

ANW Crestwood/The Paper Company
(973) 406-5000
www.anwcrestwood.com

Armour Products
(973) 427-8787
www.armourproducts.com

BasicGrey
(801) 544-1116
www.basicgrey.com

Bazzill Basics Paper Inc.
(800) 560-1610
www.bazzillbasics.com

Beacon Adhesives Inc.
(914) 699-3405
www.beaconcreates.com

Clearsnap Inc.
(800) 448-4862
www.clearsnap.com

Creative Impressions Inc.
(719) 596-4860
www.creativeimpressions.com

Die Cuts With A View
(801) 224-6766
www.diecutswithaview.com

The Dow Chemical Co.
(800) 258-2436
www.dow.com

Elmer's® Products Inc.
(800) 848-9400
www.elmers.com

Flower Soft Inc.
(877) 989-0205
www.flower-soft.com

Glue Dots International
(888) 688-7131
www.gluedots.com

Hampton Art
(800) 981-5169
www.hamptonart.com

Heidi Swapp/Advantus Corp.
(904) 482-0092
www.heidiswapp.com

Hero Arts
(800) 822-4376
www.heroarts.com

Imagination International Inc.
(541) 684-0013
www.copicmarker.com

Inkadinkado
(888) 294-3929

JustRite® Stampers
www.justritestampers.com

Kaisercraft
(888) 684-7147
www.kaisercraft.net

Making Memories
(800) 286-5263
www.makingmemories.com

Martha Stewart Crafts
www.marthastewart.com/crafts

May Arts
(203) 637-8366
www.mayarts.com

Michaels Stores Inc.
(800) MICHAELS (642-4235)
www.michaels.com

My Mind's Eye
(800) 665-5116
www.mymindseye.com

Neenah Paper Inc.
(800) 994-5993
www.neenahpaper.com

Offray
(800) 237-9425
www.offray.com

Papertrey Ink
www.papertreyink.com

Ranger Industries Inc.
(732) 389-3535
www.rangerink.com

Scor-Pal Products
(877) 629-9908
www.scor-pal.com

Spellbinders Paper Arts
(888) 547-0400
www.spellbinderspaperarts.com

Stampendous! Inc.
(800) 869-0474
www.stampendous.com

Stampin' Up!
(800) STAMP UP (782-6787)
www.stampinup.com

Taylored Expressions
www.tayloredexpressions.com

Tsukineko Inc.
(800) 769-6633
www.tsukineko.com

Wausau Paper
www.wausaupaper.com

WorldWin Papers
(888) 843-6455
www.worldwinpapers.com

Create Your Dream Wedding

Copyright © 2010 DRG, 306 East Parr Road, Berne, IN 46711

EDITOR Tanya Fox
ART DIRECTOR Brad Snow
PUBLISHING SERVICES DIRECTOR Brenda Gallmeyer
MANAGING EDITOR Barb Sprunger
ASSISTANT ART DIRECTOR Nick Pierce
COPY SUPERVISOR Michelle Beck
COPY EDITORS Mary O'Donnell, Amanda Scheerer
TECHNICAL EDITOR Marla Laux
PHOTOGRAPHY SUPERVISOR Tammy Christian
PHOTOGRAPHY Matthew Owen
PHOTOGRAPHY STYLIST Tammy Steiner
GRAPHIC ARTS SUPERVISOR Ronda Bechinski
GRAPHIC ARTIST Nicole Gage
PRODUCTION ASSISTANTS Marj Morgan, Judy Neuenschwander

Printed in the United States of America
First Printing: 2010
ISBN: 978-1-59635-283-4

AnniesAttic.com

1 2 3 4 5 6 7 8 9